John C. Calhoun and the
Secession Movement
of 1850

John C. Calhoun and the Secession Movement of 1850

BY

HERMAN V. AMES

Originally Reprinted from the Proceeding of the American Antiquarian Society for April, 1918.

 BOOKS FOR LIBRARIES PRESS
FREEPORT, NEW YORK

E340
C15 A8

First Published 1918
Reprinted 1971

INTERNATIONAL STANDARD BOOK NUMBER:
0-8369-5892-6

LIBRARY OF CONGRESS CATALOG CARD NUMBER:
71-169749

PRINTED IN THE UNITED STATES OF AMERICA
BY
NEW WORLD BOOK MANUFACTURING CO., INC.
HALLANDALE, FLORIDA 33009

JOHN C. CALHOUN AND THE SECESSION MOVEMENT OF 1850

HERMAN V. AMES

It has been truly said that "state rights apart from sectionalism have never been a serious hinderance to the progress of national unity"; on the other hand "sectionalism is by its very nature incipient disunion," as its ultimate goal is political independence for a group of states.[1] Prior to the Civil War there were numerous instances of the assertion of state rights. Almost every state in the Union at some time declared its own sovereignty but on other occasions denounced as treasonable similar declarations by other states. Only, however, when the doctrine of state rights has been laid hold of as an effective shibboleth by some particular section of the country, to give an appearance of legality to its opposition to measures of the federal government, has the doctrine threatened the integrity of the Union.

The great and outstanding sectional movement prior to the Civil War, which rallied under the banner of state rights, was due to the divergence of interests and views between the North and the South, caused by the growth of the institution of slavery. Indeed the increasing antagonism between the slave and free labor systems and States had revealed itself from time to time even in the first quarter of the Nation's history. Its sectionalizing tendency was realized by the time of the Missouri Compromise in 1820, and pointed out by several, but especially by Jefferson, when he wrote this oft-quoted passage, "This mo-

---

[1]Anson D. Morse in *Political Science Quarterly*, I, 158.

mentous question, like a fire bell in the night, a-
wakened and filled me with terror. I considered it
at once the knell of the Union. . . . A geographical
line, coinciding with a marked principle, moral and
political, once conceived and held up to the angry
passions of men will never be obliterated, and every
new irritation will make it deeper and deeper."[2]

Although the tariff was the ostensible reason for
the nullification movement in South Carolina, Calhoun
admitted in a private letter in 1830 that it was but
"the occasion, rather than the real cause of the
present unhappy state of things. The truth can no
longer be disguised that the peculiar domestic institutions of the Southern States and the consequent
direction which that and her soil and climate have
given to her industry, has placed them in regard to
taxation and appropriations in opposite relations to
the majority of the Union; against the danger of
which, if there be no protective power in the reserved
rights of the States, they must in the end be forced
to rebel or submit to having their permanent interests
sacrificed."[3]

President Jackson also recognized slavery as the
real issue. Following the settlement of the nullification controversy he wrote to a friend that "the
tariff was only the pretext, and disunion and a
southern confederacy the real object. The next
pretext will be the negro or slavery question."[4]

A striking and interesting example of the effect
of environment and the sectionalizing movement
on the thought and policy of a statesman is revealed
in the public career of John C. Calhoun, whose name
is more closely identified with state rights doctrines
than that of any other public man prior to the Civil
War.

[2]*Writings*, X, 157.
[3]Calhoun to Maxey, Sept. 11, 1830. Quoted in Bassett, *Jackson*, II, 547.
[4]Letter of May 1, 1833 to Rev. Andrew J. Crawford, given in *Congressional Globe*
36 *Cong.*, 2 *Sess.*, I, 32.

In his early life he was conspicuous for his strong nationalism and his advocacy of a liberal construction of the constitution. John Quincy Adams' contemporary estimate of Calhoun as recorded in his Diary at this period is especially noteworthy. He writes, "He is above all sectional and factional prejudices more than any other statesman of this Union with whom I ever acted."[5] The causes which led to his change of views have been variously ascribed and doubtless always will be subject to discussion. It has been claimed by some of his contemporaries, as well as by some writers of more recent times, that he was led to give up his former views to identify himself with the nullificationists who had become the dominant political party in South Carolina in the late twenties, out of consideration for his future political career and by his burning ambition to become President. While it must be admitted that Calhoun would not have been human if considerations for his political future had not had their weight, and that there is abundant evidence that, like his contemporaries Clay and Webster, he had a laudable ambition for the Presidency, nevertheless we are loathe to accept the view that such crass and selfish motives could have been the dominating ones in the mind of so great and commanding a character. Rather are we inclined to the opinion already suggested that, as a true son of the South, he was affected by his environment. He became convinced that the economic life of the South was destined to grow increasingly divergent from that of the North, and that the interests identified with and resulting from the institution of slavery would lead to its permanently being in the minority in the general government of the country. He, therefore, was led seriously to consider the means by which the peculiar interests of his section could be safe-guarded, while at the same time the Union, which he loved could be preserved. Hence

[5]*Memoirs*, V, 361.

he laid hold with eagerness upon the doctrine of
nullification as the device by which the rights and
interests of the minority were to be preserved in the
Union. The theory was an attempt to devise a
theoretical reconciliation between the most complete
state sovereignty and the existence of a general
government. Shortly after drafting the South Carolina Exposition of 1828, he writes to a private corre-
spondent, "To preserve our Union on the fair basis of
equality, on which alone it can stand, and to transmit
the blessings of liberty to the remotest posterity is
the first great object of all my exertions."[6]
  If this is a correct explanation of Calhoun's reason-
ing, we can understand why the doctrine of nullification appealed to him; first, because it reconciled
his devotion to the Union as well as to his state and
section; and secondly, it enabled him honestly to
declare, as he did declare, that it was the great
conserving feature of our system of government.[7]
The right of secession, which, since the establishment
of the government under the Constitution, had been
held from time to time in the North as well as in
the South as a theoretical possibility, was reserved
by Calhoun's Exposition as a last resort.
  The acceptance of the view just advanced of
Calhoun's motives will go far in explaining his
subsequent course. Although he championed southern interests, he restrained the radicals of his state
and section for nearly two decades longer, until at
last he became convinced that the interests of the
two sections were so irreconcilable that the Union
ought not to be preserved except at the price of
specific constitutional concessions.[8] Apparently, the
year 1847 marks the date when Calhoun, alarmed by
the aggressiveness of the northern advocates of the

[6]Calhoun's Correspondence, *American Historical Association Report*, 1899, II, 269–
270.
[7]Calhoun, *Works*, VI, 50, 123.
[8]Beverley Tucker's letter, March 25, 1850. *William and Mary Quarterly*, XVIII, 45.
See *post*.

Wilmot Proviso, deemed it high time to arouse the
South "to calculate the value of the Union." In a
private letter, dated March 19, 1847, he writes,
"The time has come when it (the slavery question)
must be brought to a final decision."[9]

The part that Calhoun played in the sectional
agitation during the next three years, the last of his
life, and especially his part in launching and promoting
the project for a Southern Convention, as also the
history of the movement for such a Convention of the
Southern States, which was to demand protection
for the rights of that section in the Union, or to
concert measures for secession from the Union, is
the theme of the remainder of this paper. The idea
of a Southern Convention, however, was not new.[10]
It had been proposed as early as 1844, both at the
time of the Texas agitation and in connection with
the tariff agitation of that year. The project at
that time found considerable support in South
Carolina both in the press and with the public, as
fiery and radical speeches, resolutions, and toasts
threatening disunion testify. The Hon. R. Barnwell
Rhett, Calhoun's colleague in the United States
Senate, especially championed the measure. The
movement, however, met with general opposition in
the other Southern States and Calhoun and his
friends opposed it, favoring a more astute policy and
awaiting the results of the Presidential election.
The resulting election of Polk led to the abandonment
of the project, even by its former advocates.

The demand of the North that slavery should be
excluded from all the new territory that it was
expected would be acquired as a result of the Mexican
War revived the sectional issue. Calhoun now takes

[9]Correspondence, 720. See also letter to a member of the Alabama Legislature, Benton, *Thirty Years View*, II, 698.

[10]Louisiana,February 20,1837,had proposed one "to determine the best possible means to obtain peaceably if they can, forcibly if they must, that respect for their institutions to which they are entitled by the enactments of the Federal compact," etc. *Acts of Louisiana*, 1837, 18, 19.

the lead. Following the adoption of the Wilmot Proviso by the House of Representatives for the second time, on February 15, 1847, he delivered a speech in the Senate in which he denounced the Proviso and summoned the South to repudiate compromise and stand upon her rights. At the same time he presented a set of resolutions containing a new doctrine that Congress can impose no restriction upon slavery in the territories.[11] They became known as "the Platform of the South." Although these resolutions were not pressed to a vote, the principles underlying them were generally adopted by the southern Democrats, and soon found expression in the resolutions of several of the Southern State legislatures, notably by Virginia, which was the first to adopt them.[12] Apparently, Calhoun was fully convinced that it was high time that something should be done to unite the South in order to preserve her interests in the Union. In a private letter of this period he wrote that instead of shunning, we ought to court the issue with the North on the slavery question. I would even go one step further, and add that it is our duty due to ourselves, to the Union and our political institutions to force the issue on the North."[13]

Partially abandoning his previous policy of restraining the radicals in South Carolina, he threw himself into the movement to arouse the people. On his return from Washington early in March, he was greeted with great enthusiasm by the Mayor and Council of Charleston and a mass meeting of the citizens. This meeting, after listening to Calhoun's plea for the union of the South on the slavery issue regardless of party ties, adopted a strong report and resolutions similar to those that he had presented in Congress.[14]

---

[11]Calhoun, *Works*, IV, 339–349.

[12]March 8, 1847, *Acts of Virginia*, 1846–47, 236.

[13]Benton, *Thirty Years View*, II, 698.

[14]Calhoun's Speech, March 9, 1847, *Works*, IV, 382–396; *Niles' Register*, LXII, 73–75; Calhoun, *Correspondence*, 718, 720; McMaster, VII, 486–489, 494–495.

Some both in and out of the State suspected that Calhoun was playing politics.[15] President Polk in particular held this view. Following the former's efforts to secure the signatures of prominent southerners to an address to the people of the United States on the subject of slavery and the making of this question a test in the next Presidential election, Polk records his condemnation in his Diary under date of April 6, 1847. "Mr. Calhoun has become perfectly desperate in his aspiration to the Presidency, and has seized upon this sectional question as the only means of sustaining himself in his present fallen condition, and that such an agitation of the slavery question was not only unpatriotic and mischievous, but wicked. I now entertain a worse opinion of Mr. Calhoun than I have ever done before. He is wholly selfish, and I am satisfied has no patriotism. A few years ago he was the author of nullification and threatened to dissolve the Union on account of the tariff. During my administration the reduction of duties which he desired has been obtained, and he can no longer complain. No sooner is this done than he selects slavery upon which to agitate the country, and blindly mounts the topic as a hobby."[16]

Calhoun's suggestion was not sufficiently encouraged, so the proposed address was not issued at this time. The presidential campaign of 1848 led to a postponement of the issue. Calhoun endeavored to maintain a neutral position during the contest. His correspondence for the year 1848, however, shows that he was carefully considering the utility of a Southern Convention. In a speech delivered in

---

[15]See note, next page.

[16]*Diary*, II, 458–9. James H. Hammond writes to W. G. Simms, March 21, 1847, that he has just read Calhoun's Charleston speech. His object is to gain Southern votes for himself for President. Every one in S. Carolina will see this. It will be said that he agitates the slavery question for selfish purposes—"South Carolina under present auspices can do nothing if she puts herself foremost but divide the South and insure disastrous defeat." *Hammond Manuscript*, Vol. 13, Library of Congress. For this and other references to the Hammond collection, I am indebted to Mr. Philip M. Hamer, a member of the Graduate School, University of Pennsylvania.

Charleston, August 20, he intimated more clearly than in any previous public utterance that the question of southern union and secession might soon be a vital one.[17] The press and public meetings throughout the State favored resistance and some urged that South Carolina should take the lead in calling a Southern Convention. As will appear later, Calhoun, while sympathizing with the movement, believed for reasons of expediency it should be initiated in one of the other states, and so he exercised to some extent a restraining influence. On the assembling of the legislature in November of 1848, Governor Johnson in his message, while stating that the present time, owing to the election of Taylor, a Southern man as President was not propitious for action, declared that "unity of time and concert of action are indispensable to success, and a Southern Convention is the most direct and practical means of obtaining it."[18] The legislature on December 15, after a visit of Calhoun to Columbia, on his way to Washington,[19] unanimously adopted resolutions which were apparently in harmony with his wishes. These declared "that the time for discussion had passed, and that this General Assembly is prepared to co-operate with her sister states in resisting the application of the principles of the Wilmot Proviso to such territory at any and all hazard."[20]

On the re-opening of Congress after the election of 1848, Calhoun renewed his effort to secure the issuing of a Southern Address, this time with more success, as the situation in Washington favored his project

[17]Speech in Charleston, *New York Semi-Weekly Tribune*, August 28, 1848. Toombs writes Crittenden, September 27, 1847, "Calhoun stands off too, in order to make a Southern party all his own on slavery in the new Territories. Poor old dotard, to suppose he could get a party now on any terms! Hereafter treachery itself will not trust him." Correspondence of Toombs, Stephens, and Cobb, *American Historical Association Report*, 1911, II, 129.

[18]November 27, 1848, *Journal of Senate of S. Carolina*, 1848, 26; *Niles' Register*, LXXIV, 368; Calhoun, *Correspondence*, 1184.

[19]*South Carolina Senate Journal*, 1848, 61.

[20]*Report and Resolutions of South Carolina*, 1848, 147.

inasmuch as the slavery question had re-appeared in Congress in several different measures. The sectionalizing effect of the renewed agitation soon revealed itself. As a result of this, and of Calhoun's labors, a gathering of sixty-nine Southern members of Congress, drawn from both parties, assembled on the evening of December 23, 1848, to determine upon a common policy for the South. Calhoun and the radical Democrats directed the movement. It was commonly believed in Washington, wrote Horace Mann, "that Mr. Calhoun was resolved on a dissolution of the Union."[21] The attempt was made to unite the representatives of both parties, but it failed of success. President Polk threw the weight of his influence against it. It soon appeared that the Whigs had only entered the conference in order to try to control or defeat the movement.[22] "An Address of the Southern Delegates in Congress to their Constituents" was drafted by Calhoun, in which he arraigned the North for their infraction of the Constitution in regard to fugitive slaves and their general course relative to slavery. It denied that Congress had any jurisdiction over slavery in the territories, and it called upon the South to unite, to subordinate party ties, and to prepare to protect itself. "If you become united, " it read, "and prove yourself in earnest, the North will be brought to pause, and to a calculation of consequences; and that may lead to a change of measures and to the adoption of a course of policy that may quietly and peaceably terminate this long conflict between the two sections. If it should not, nothing would remain for you but to stand up immovably in defence of rights involving your all, your property, prosperity, equality, liberty, and safety."[23]

---

[21]*Life and Works of Horace Mann*, 273.

[22]See Letters of Toombs to John J. Crittenden, *American Historical Association Report*, 1911, II, 139, 141.

[23]Calhoun, *Works*, VI, 290–313; *Niles*, LXXV, 84–88.

But the Whigs were not prepared to abandon their party affiliations. As Toombs wrote Crittenden, "We had a regular flare up in the last meeting, and at the call of Calhoun I told them briefly what we were at. I told him (Calhoun) that the union of the South was neither possible nor desirable until we were ready to dissolve the Union. That we certainly did not intend to advise the people now to look any where else than to their own government for the prevention of apprehended evils."[24] Alexander H. Stephens tried to prevent action by the caucus, but failed in this. An attempt to substitute an address drawn by Senator Berrien, directed to the "People of the whole Country" and appealing to the patriotism and fairness of the North, failed by a small margin[25] and the Calhoun Address slightly modified was adopted and issued on January 22, 1849, but only two Whigs were numbered among its forty-eight signers. Only about one third of the southern representatives signed.

Owing to the attitude of the Whigs, the effect of the address was greatly weakened. In fact Toombs declared "We have completely foiled Calhoun in his miserable attempt to form a Southern Party."[26] Calhoun, however, in a letter to his daughter two days after the Address was issued, expressed satisfaction. He writes, "My address was adopted by a decided majority. . . . It is a decided triumph under the circumstances. The administration threw all its weight against us, and added it to the most rabid of the Whigs. . . . . The South is more aroused than I ever saw it on the subject."[27] Polk's Diary bears out Calhoun's statement of the administration's hostility to their movement. The President records an interview with Calhoun on January

---

[24]Coleman, *Life of John J. Crittenden*, I, 335–336.
[25]*Niles*, LXXV, 101–104.
[26]Coleman, *Crittenden*, I, 335.
[27]*Correspondence*, 762.

16, 1840, and notes, "He (Calhoun) proposed no
plan of adjusting the difficulty (territorial), but
insisted that the aggression of the North upon the
South should be resisted and that the time had come
for action. I became perfectly satisfied that he did
not desire that Congress should settle the question
at the present session and that he desired to influence
the North upon the subject, whether from personal
or patriotic views it is not difficult to determine.
I was firm and decided in my conversation with him,
intending to let him understand distinctly that I
gave no countenance to any movement which tended
to violence or the disunion of the states."[28]

Just before the final meeting of the caucus, Polk
was so disturbed that he conferred with his Cabinet
on the matter and informed them that he "thought
it was wholly unjustifiable for southern members of
Congress, when a fair prospect was presented of
settling the whole question, to withhold their co-
operation, and instead of aiding in effecting such an
adjustment, to be meeting in a sectional caucus and
publishing an address to influence the country."
"I added," he records, "that I feared there were a
few southern men who had become so excited that
they were indifferent to the preservation of the
Union." "I stated that I put my face alike against
southern agitators and northern fanatics and should
do everything in my power to allay excitement by
adjusting the question of slavery and preserving the
Union."[29] It was agreed that each member of the
Cabinet should be active in seeing members of
Congress, and urge them to support the bill to admit
California at once as a state. Polk promised to use
his influence with members, and records in his Diary:
—"This is an unusual step for the Executive to take,
but the emergency demands it. It may be the only
means of allaying a fearful sectional excitement and

[28]*Diary*, IV, 288.
[29]*Diary*, IV, 299.

14

of preserving the Union, and therefore I think upon high public consideration it is justified."[30]

Through the administration's influence, some of the Democrats joined the southern Whigs in refusing to support the address, yet the South Carolina legislature, as previously stated, had declared that it was prepared to co-operate with other Southern States in resisting the extension of the Wilmot Proviso to the new territory. In the course of the next few weeks, the Democratic legislatures in Virginia, Florida, and Missouri adopted resolutions of similar tenor, and even the Whig legislature of North Carolina joined in denouncing the proposed restrictive legislation and suggested the extension of the Missouri Compromise line to the new territory.[31] Virginia took more radical action by providing for a special session of the legislature, should Congress pass the obnoxious laws. In several of the other states, although there was no legislative action, there was a renewal of popular agitation. While the sentiment in both Georgia and Alabama was divided on the Southern Address, the Wilmot Proviso was emphatically condemned by both political parties. In Georgia, Governor Town, who had declared himself in favor of resisting the Wilmot Proviso to the limit, was re-elected, and the Democrats gained control of the legislature for the first time in several years. In Alabama the Democrats also made substantial gains. Moreover, Mississippi, as we shall presently see, took up with zeal the proposal for the Southern Convention.

Calhoun had not ventured in the "Address of the Southern Delegates" to explicitly propose a Southern Convention, but we know he had entertained the possibility of one for some time. More than a year previously he had stated in a confidential letter that

[30]*Diary*, IV, 300.

[31]*Senate Misc.*, 30 *Congress*, 2 *session*, I, Nos. 48, 51, II, Nos. 54, 58; *Senate Misc.*, 31 *Congress*, 1 *session*, I, No. 24.

such a Convention was "indispensable."[32] Within a few weeks after the southern caucus, his personal correspondence to political friends in several states shows that he was actively, although quietly, urging the idea of a southern Convention and outlining the plan of action. Thus we find him writing to John H. Means, shortly afterward chosen Governor of South Carolina. "I am of the impression that the time is near at hand when the South will have to choose between disunion and submission. I think so, because I see little prospect of arresting the aggression of the North. If any thing can do it, it would be for the South to present with an unbroken front to the North the alternative of dissolving the partnership or of ceasing on their part to violate our rights. . . . But it will be impossible to present such a front, except by means of a Convention of Southern States. That, and that only could speak for the whole, and present authoritatively to the North the alternative, which to choose. If such a presentation should fail to save the Union, by arresting the aggression of the North and causing our rights and the stipulation of the Constitution in our favor to be respected, it would afford proof conclusive that it could not be saved, and that nothing was left us, but to save ourselves. Having done all we could to save the Union, we would then stand justified before God and man to dissolve a partnership which had proved inconsistent with our safety, and, of course, destructive of the object which mainly induced us to enter into it. Viewed in this light, a Convention of the South is an indispensable means to discharge a great duty we owe to our partners in the Union: that is, to warn them in the most solemn manner that if they do not desist from aggressions and cease to disregard our rights and stipulations of the Constitution, the duty we owe to ourselves and our posterity would compel us

---

[32]Benton, *Thirty Years View*, II, 698–700. Letter of Wilson Lumkin to Calhoun, November 18, 1847. *Correspondence*, 1135–1139.

to dissolve forever the partnership with them. But should its warning voice fail to save the Union, it would in that case prove the most efficient of all means for saving ourselves."[33]

Scarcely more than a month after this letter was written, in accordance with a plan privately suggested by Calhoun, and publicly favored by district and parish meetings in various parts of South Carolina, a Convention of delegates assembled at Columbia, May 14–15, 1849. After approving the Southern Address and the action of the state government, it called for a special session of the legislature to take action in case any of the proposed obnoxious legislation should be passed by Congress. This Convention also appointed five prominent men as a Central Committee of Vigilance and Safety to correspond with the other states to promote concert of action, and to perfect the organization of the state—thus fully accepting Calhoun's program.[34]

It was desired, however, that some state other than South Carolina should take the lead. Mississippi was the first to respond under the stimulus of Mr. Calhoun's letters.[35] In May, 1849, an informal meeting of prominent citizens was held at Jackson to protest against southern exclusion from the territories. This gathering issued a call for the voters of the several counties to choose delegates to a State Convention to be held at Jackson in October "to consider the threatening relations between the North and the South." A copy of their resolutions was sent to Mr. Calhoun with the request that he advise the promoters of the movement the proper course for the Convention to take. Calhoun replied in a letter addressed to Col. C. S. Tarpley, dated July 9, 1849, outlining the course that it was desirable

---

[33]Calhoun to John H. Means, *Correspondence*, 765, 766.

[34]*National Era*, May 24, 1849. *National Intelligencer*, May 24 and 26, 1849.

[35]D. T. Herndon in *Alabama Hist. Society Transactions*, V, 204–208; Cleo Hearon in *Publications of Miss. Hist. Society*, XIV, ch. II and III.

to take. His letter was in part as follows:[36] "In my opinion there is but one thing that holds out the promise of saving both ourselves and the Union: and that is a Southern Convention; and that, if much longer delayed, cannot. It ought to have been held this fall, and ought not to be delayed beyond another year; all our movements ought to look to that result. For that purpose every southern state ought to be organized, with a central committee and one in each county. Ours is already. It is indispensable to produce concert and prompt action. In the meantime, firm and resolute resolutions ought to be adopted by yours and such meetings as may take place before the assembling of the legislature in the fall. They, when they meet, ought to take up the subject in the most solemn and impressive manner.

"The great object of a Southern Convention should be, to put forth in a solemn manner the causes of our grievances in an address to other states, and to admonish them, in a solemn manner, of the consequences which must follow, if they should not be redressed, and to take measures preparatory to it, in case they should not be. The call should be addressed to all those who are desirous to save the Union and our institutions, and who, in the alternative, should it be forced on us, of submission or dissolving the *partnership*, would prefer the latter. No state could better take the lead in this great conservative movement than yours." Calhoun wrote a similar letter to Senator Henry S. Foote, August 2, 1849,[37] to which Foote replied a few days before the Mississippi Convention met, stating, "I am gratified to have it within my power to inform you that several leading gentlemen of both the two great political parties in Mississippi have promised me at

---

[36]"*The Southron*," Jackson, Miss., published Mr. Calhoun's letter May 24, 1850. Copied in *National Daily Intelligencer*, June 4, 1850, also *Cong. Globe*, 32 *Cong.* 1 *sess.* *Appendix* 52.

[37]*National Era*, June 12, 1851.

our approaching convention to act upon your sug
gestion relative to the recommendation of a Southern
Convention."[38]

His suggestions were explicitly followed. The
State formally took the lead, a central committee
was organized and local committees were appointed
in the counties, "firm and determined resolutions"
were adopted by the October Convention. These
condemned the policy of Congress, and appointed a
committee of seven which issued "An Address to the
Southern States," inviting them to send delegates
to a Convention to be held at Nashville, June 3, 1850,
"with the view and the hope of arresting the course
of aggression, and, if not practicable then to concen-
trate the South in will and understanding, and action,"
"and as the possible ultimate resort the call by the
legislatures of the assailed States of still more solemn
Conventions,—to deliberate, speak, and act with
all the sovereign power of the people. Should, in
the result, such Conventions be called and held,
they may look to a like regularly constituted convention of all the assailed States, to provide in the
last resort for their separate welfare, by the formation
of a compact and a union that will afford protection
to their liberties and their rights."[39]

Calhoun's connection with the movement was not
generally known but was suspected.[40] Following

[38]Letter of September 25, 1849, Calhoun, *Correspondence*, 1204. See also letter
from A. Hutchinson to Calhoun of October 5, 1849, *Ibid*, 1206.

[39]For address and resolutions, *Congressional Globe*, 31, *Cong.* I, *Sess.*, I, 578; 579, 942.

[40]Senator Foote in a speech February 8, 1850, denied that the Mississippi movement
was instigated by South Carolina. *Congressional Globe*. 31 *Cong.* 1 *sess. Appendix*
100. In December, 1851, however, he acknowledged "that it was through me, in the
first instance that Mr. Calhoun succeeded in instigating the incipient movement in
Mississippi, which led to the calling of the Nashville Convention." *Ibid*, 32 *Cong.*
1 *sess. Appendix*, 52. A few days later he stated that he had not known of Mr. Calhoun's
letter to Mr. Tarpley and to others until recently, and added "the letters that I have
seen, according generally with this one (Tarpley) satisfied my mind that the *modus
operandi* of the Convention was more or less marked out by his great intellect." *Cong.
Globe*, 32 *Cong.* 1 *sess.* 134–135.

Daniel Wallace was sent by Governor Seabrook of South Carolina as a special agent
to attend the Mississippi Convention. In a confidential letter he reports that he noted
there the influence of "our own old statesman." (Calhoun). See Report of D. Wallace,
Special Agent from South Carolina to Mississippi, in collection of letters of W. B. Seabrook in the Library of Congress. For Wallace's denial that he was an agent of South
Carolina, see references cited by A. C. Cole. The South and the Right of Secession, in
Mississippi Valley Historical Review, I, 377, note 2.

his speech in Congress, March 4, 1850, just before his death, it was asserted. Thus the Fayetteville, (N. C.) *Observer* declared: "The proposition to hold such a convention was first authoritatively made in Mississippi. But we presume nobody is so green as to imagine that it originated there. No, we have no shadow of doubt that the action of Mississippi was prompted from South Carolina, and now in Mr. Calhoun's speech we have a revelation of the purpose for which the Convention is to assemble. It is to demand impracticable and impossible concessions, with no hope of their being granted, and with a purpose and declaration that if not granted the South will secede from the Union." His letter to Colonel Tarpley was not made public until after his death, shortly before the assembling of the Nashville Convention.

Calhoun followed the progress of events with great interest and urged his correspondents in Georgia, Alabama, and South Carolina to see that their states supported the Mississippi movement.[41] He writes James H. Hammond, "As to myself, I lose no opportunity, when I can act with propriety, to give the great cause an impulse. . . . . I have made it a point to throw off no one. Let us be one is my advice to all parties in the South. . . . . The time for action has come. If the South is to be saved, now is the time."[42]

His own State Government was the first to respond. Governor Seabrook's message to the legislature, when it assembled the last of November (1849) reviewed the slavery agitation. He predicted that "the enactment of any one of the contemplated measures of hostility would probably, if not certainly, result in severing the political ties that now unite us. . . . . the South has at last been aroused from

[41]*Correspondence*, 762, 769, 773, 775, 778. Letters to Calhoun, *Ibid*, 1195, 1196, 1199-1202, 1210-1212.

[42]Letter of January 4, 1850, *Correspondence*, 779.

its criminal lethargy to a knowledge of the dangers of its position. For the first time in our political history, party affinities are becoming merged in the high obligation of co-operation for the sake of safety, or for participation in a common fate." He concluded by recommending the Southern Convention as proposed by the people of Mississippi. This recommendation was endorsed by the legislature, meeting as a caucus, December 12, 1849, and the election of delegates was provided for.[43] They also adopted the measures recommended by the May Convention.

Calhoun's fondest hope for the union of the men of the South of both political parties seemed about to be realized. Whigs vied with Democrats in declaring that southern rights were in universal danger, and that only a united and bold front would prevent the enactment of measures that would force the disruption of the Union. Southern men and the southern press were even seriously considering the value of the Union and the advantages of its dissolution.

On the assembling of Congress in December of 1849, Alexander H. Stephens of Georgia, a leading southern Whig wrote "I find the feeling among the southern members for a dissolution of the Union—if the anti-slavery measures should be pressed to extremity—is becoming more general than at first. Men are now beginning to talk of it seriously, who, twelve months ago, hardly permitted themselves to think of it."[44] Calhoun a little later wrote, "The southern members are more determined and bold than I ever saw them. Many avow themselves to be disunionists, and a still greater number admit that there is little hope for any remedy short of it."[45]

---

[43] *The Tri-Weekly South Carolinian*, December 8, 1849.

[44] Johnson and Brown, *Life of Alexander H. Stephens*, 239.

[45] January 12, 1850, Calhoun, *Correspondence*, 780, also December 8, 31, 1849; *Ibid*, 776, 778.

Similar opinions were expressed in many southern papers. The *Richmond Enquirer* of February 12 declared, "The two great political parties of the country have ceased to exist in the Southern States, so far as the present slavery issue is concerned. United they will prepare, consult, combine, for prompt and decisive action. With united voices—we are compelled to make a few exceptions—they proclaim, in the language of the Virginia resolution, passed a day since, the preservation of the Union if we can, the preservation of our own rights if we cannot. This is the temper of the South; this is the temper becoming the inheritors of rights acquired for freemen by the hand of freemen. 'Thus far shalt thou come, and no farther,' or else the proud waves of Northern aggression shall float the wreck of the Constitution."[46]

A communication in the Columbia (S. C.) *Telegraph*, February 15, 1850, reads: "My idea is, first, to perfect the Union of the South, now so happily in progress. A year ago I thought the South was doomed, it seemed so dead to the true situation, mouthing after the lessons of miserable demagogues the sounding devices of party. But that day is past. There are no more Whigs, no more Democrats —there is but one party, 'The party of the South.' The South is aroused, her banner is on the outer wall, and the cry is still 'they come, they come,' 'Let the good work go on.' Second, to dissolve the Union immediately, form a Southern Confederacy, and the possession by force of most of all the territories suitable for slavery, which would include all south of the northern latitude of Missouri."[47]

Even *The Richmond Republican*, a conservative Whig paper, said editorially, "We are afraid these men will find the South is in earnest when it is too late. . . . . It is melancholy to contemplate such a state of things; for whatever Northern citizens

---

[46]Quoted in *National Intelligencer*, February 16, 1850.
[47]Quoted in *National Intelligencer*, February 21, 1850.

may believe, or affect to believe, every Southern man knows that to persist in those measures which form the principal point of Northern policy upon the subject of slavery, will result in a dissolution of the Union."[48]

Robert Toombs, a Whig representative from Georgia, wrote "When I came to Washington, I found the whole Whig party expecting to pass the Proviso, and Taylor would not veto it . . . . I saw General Taylor, and talked fully with him, and while he stated he had given and would give no pledges either way about the Proviso, he gave me clearly to understand that if it was passed he would sign it. My course instantly became fixed. I would not hesitate to oppose the Proviso, even to the extent of a dissolution of the Union."[49] He, therefore, believed that the Whigs should join with the southern Democrats in presenting a determined resistance to this obnoxious measure.

Stephens's letters from December to early in February show a similar determination as well as despair of the preservation of the Union. Thus he writes his brother on January 21: "I see no hope to the South from the Union. I do not believe much in resolutions, anyway. I am a good deal like Troup in this particular. If I were now in the legislature, I should introduce bills reorganizing the militia, for the establishment of a military school the encouragement of the formation of volunteer companies, the creation of arsenals, of an armory, and an establishment for making gunpowder. In these lies our defence. I tell you the argument is exhausted, and if the South does not intend to be overrun with anti-slavery doctrines, they must, before no distant day, stand by their arms. My mind is made up; I am for the fight, if the country will back me. And, if not, we had better have no 'Resolutions'

[48]Quoted in *National Intelligencer*, February 2, 1850.
[49]Coleman, *Life of John J. Crittenden*, 365, letter dated April 25, 1850.

and no gasconade. They will but add to our degradation."[50] The *National Intelligencer*, a Whig paper published in Washington, in the leading editorial February 2, entitled, "The Evil of the Day," confirmed this view of the attitude of the southern Whigs. "What is most alarming of all," it declared, "is the fact that gentlemen who have ever heretofore been most conservative and even thoroughly Whig, are to be found still more excited than those who have been habitually railers against the North, and undervaluers of the Union."

In the meantime the movement for the Nashville Convention was taken up in the other southern legislatures as they assembled. The legislatures of Virginia, Georgia, Florida, Alabama, Mississippi, Texas, and Arkansas voted respectively that their states would be represented, but not without opposition in some states, and considerable difference of opinion in regard to the methods to be employed for the choice of delegates. In general, the Whigs desired election by the people, the Democrats by the legislature. As a result there were a variety of methods adopted.

In some states all the delegates were chosen by the legislature, in others a part were so chosen to represent the state at large, and the remainder by the district system. In a few states, where the choice was left to the people it resulted in only a partial representation as was true of Virginia, Texas, and Arkansas. The legislature of Tennessee, Louisiana and several of the border states refused to indorse the Convention, and from only one of these, Tennessee, were any representatives present at Nashville.[51] Four of the state legislatures, namely, Georgia, Alabama, Mississippi, and Virginia also authorized the calling of a state Convention in case the Wilmot Proviso or similar

---

[50]Johnson and Brown, *Stephens*, 245. See also letter of February 13, 1850 to Jas. Thomas, *American Hist. Assoc. Report*, 1911, II, 184.

[51]Cole, *The Whig Party in the South*, 158–162, 170–171. D. T. Herndon, The Nashville Convention of 1850, in *Transactions of the Alabama Historical Society*, V, 213–216.

obnoxious measures were adopted by Congress. Mississippi added an appropriation of $220,000 as a contingency fund.

From the moment of the introduction of Clay's resolutions, the southern Whig sentiment began to change, and it was soon evident that the majority of their numbers were ready to accept the admission of California, if the Wilmot Proviso was not applied to the rest of the Mexican cession. It was otherwise with the southern Democrats. On the 4th of March, Calhoun's speech, the last great effort of his life, was presented to the Senate.[52] The scene was a dramatic one. The knowledge that the veteran statesman and great champion of southern rights was to emerge from his sick room to present his views on the crisis of the hour was sufficient to crowd the Senate Chamber. Too ill to deliver the speech himself, it was read by Senator Mason of Virginia. Calhoun, pale and emaciated sat with eyes partially closed, listening to the delivery of his last appeal and solemn warning. "A sombre hue pervaded the whole speech," wrote Senator Cass. It was, indeed, clear that the author, conscious of his approaching end, was oppressed with anxious forebodings of the disruption of the Union. He declared that the Compromise proposed could not save the Union. This could be done only by the North giving to the South equal rights in the territories, by ceasing to agitate the slavery question and by consenting to an amendment to the Constitution which would restore to the South the power to protect herself. The amendment as explained in a posthumous essay provided for the election of two Presidents, one from each section, each to have a veto on all legislation.[53]

This extreme demand did not command the support of the southern Whigs, and Webster's "Seventh of March Speech" did much to reassure them,[54] and the

---

[52]*Congressional Globe*, 31 *Cong.* 1 *Sess.*, I, 451–455; *Works*, IV, 542–573.

[53]*A Discourse on the Constitution and Government of the United States.*

southern press in general applauded it; while many
condemned Calhoun's remedy as impracticable. Thus
the *Virginia Free Press* declares: "The necessity
of the Convention, if it ever existed is now at an end.
. . . . Since the delivery of Mr. Webster's speech
the great body of the people feel a confidence that the
agitating and exciting question of the day will be
amicably settled and the clouds which lately lowered
so darkly over the Union will be dispelled.[55] Even
the radical *Charleston Mercury* says: "With such a
spirit as Mr. Webster has shown, it no longer seems
impossible to bring this sectional contest to a close,
and we feel now, or the first time since Congress
met, a hope that it may be adjusted.[56] The *New
Orleans Bee* declared that "the public sentiment of
nine-tenths of the people of the South will rebuke
the opinion of Mr. Calhoun and stamp it as calumny
upon the slave holding part of the community."[57]
The change in the attitude of the press in regard to
the Nashville Convention was general, but particu-
larly marked in the case of the Whig papers. The
Wilmington Chronicle states that of sixty papers
from ten slave-holding states from Maryland to
Louisiana, not more than one quarter take decided
ground for a Southern Convention. "The rest are
either strongly opposed to it, doubt its utility or are
silent on the subject."[58] The Jackson (Mississippi)
Southron had at first supported the movement, but
by March it had grown luke-warm and before the
Convention assembled, decidedly opposed to it.
The last of May it said, "not a Whig paper in the

---

[54]Toombs in letter of March 22, 1850 to Linton Stephens wrote:—"We have a tolerable
prospect for a proper settlement of the slavery question. I should think it a strong
prospect if it were not that the Calhoun wing of the South seem to desire no settlement
and may perhaps go against any adjustment which would likely pass." *American
Historical Association Report*, 1911, II, 188.

[55]*National Intelligencer*, March 18 and 23.

[56]*Ibid.*

[57]*National Intelligencer*, March 11.

[58]*National Intelligencer*, March 19.

state approves."[59] The Savannah *Republican* early
in the year seemed to be in doubt what course to
recommend; by the latter part of March it had grown
fearful "that evil men may use it for their own
purposes," especially so since Calhoun's speech.
By the end of May it pronounces against such a
sectional assembly pending the action of Congress.[60]

On the other hand leading Democrats and several
of the influential party papers tried to check the
rising tide of union sentiment and to urge the Convention forward. A meeting of southern Senators
was held in Washington on April 16th, at which all
except four were present. They unanimously recognized the importance of the Convention being held.[61]
The Columbus *Sentinel* (Georgia) declared "Let the
Convention be held and let the undivided voice of
the South go forth, ... from the deliberations
of that Convention, declaring our determination to
resist even to civil war, and we shall then and not
till then hope for a respectful recognition of our
equality and rights."[62]

In South Carolina many declared openly in favor of
secession. Thus the Fairfield *Herald* of May 1
states its views: "The time for the Southern Convention is nigh at hand, and with its approach con-
flicting opinions harass the mind. The question has
been frequently asked, with all seriousness, what will
be the probable action of the Convention? We have
hoped, and we still desire, that the Convention will
assume a decided position and declare to the North
that there is a line established beyond which, if they
dare trespass, a revolution shall be the consequence.
Further than this, we anxiously pray that the Convention may entertain the proposition of the formation
of a Southern Confederacy. The Union, as it now

[59]Compare *Southron*, September 21, October 5, 1849, March 11, 15, 22, April 5, 19,
May 24, 31, June 7, 1850.
[60]*Savannah Republican*, March 21, 22, May 20, 1850.
[61]*Montgomery Advertiser*, April 16, 1850.
[62]*National Intelligencer*, March 11.

exists, has proved a curse and not a blessing. It
has been made the means of catering to northern
taste and inclinations, robbing from the southern
planter his pittance to pander to the craving pro-
pensities of northern leeches. In the language of
the Wilmington *Aurora* (which we unhesitatingly
endorse) we would say to our delegates, who will
shortly leave for the Convention, if they intend to
furnish us with *barren addresses* merely, they had
better stay at home."[63]

Such utterances as these led several of the Whig
delegates who had been chosen to the Convention,
especially in Georgia, to decline to attend on the
ground that the movement had not the support of
the people as shown by the small vote cast, and
because they were opposed to anything looking
toward disunion.[64] "They saw," said the *Southron*,
"that South Carolina and portions of the loco foco
party in other states were determined to press the
consideration at the Nashville Convention the propriety of the treasonable project of disunion."[65]
Some of the Whigs, however, decided to attend to
prevent extreme measures. William M. Murphy,
one of the delegates at large from Alabama, published
an open letter stating his reasons. "It is said that
the object of the Convention is to dissolve the Union;
if this be true no earthly power should prevent my
attendance—to prevent that awful calamity."[66]

Chief Justice Sharkey and the Mississippi Whigs,
however, attended, and the former both before the
Convention met, [67] and in his speech from the President's chair in that body, denied that the object of
the originators of the movement was to dissolve the
Union but to obtain relief from the "violations of
the Constitution which the North had made."

---

[63]*National Intelligencer*, March 10, 1850.

[64]*National Intelligencer*, June 1850. Especially letter of Ex-Representative Jas. A
Meriweather of Georgia. Augusta Chronicle quoted in *National Intelligencer*, May
7, 1850. *Savannah Republican*, quoted in Philadelphia *Public Ledger*, April 2, 1850.

[65]Jackson *Southron*, May 31.

"The Convention had not been called to prevent, but to perpetuate union."[68]

As we have seen, Calhoun was largely responsible for the assembling of the Southern Convention, and it is apparent that he had hoped to guide its proceedings. Indeed he had suggested, as late as the middle of February, that "at least two members from each of the delegations should visit Washington on their way to Nashville, in order to consult fully with the members from the South that are true to her."[69] Had he lived doubtless he would have exercised great influence in directing its work.[70] From his correspondence of the last few months of his life, as well as from articles in papers inspired by him, we are able to form an excellent idea of what he hoped the Convention would accomplish. In a letter to the editor of his organ the *South Carolinian*, Calhoun wrote early in the winter that "the great object of the Convention is to make a solemn statement of the wrongs of the South and to appeal to the North to desist. Further, in case the latter should refuse to alter its course, to devise some means of action."[71] It is probable that he intended the Convention to embody in its demands the indispensable guarantees that he had presented in his last speech in Congress. This was the view taken by Senator Foote, who the day following the presentation of Calhoun's speech protested in the Senate against the demand for amendments to the Constitution as a *sine qua non* on the part of the South. Calhoun immediately replied disclaiming having said anything about a *sine qua non* but added, "I will

[68]Montgomery *Alabama Journal*, May 22.

[67]Letter of April 4 in *National Intelligencer*, April 27. Senator Foote in a speech February 14, 1850, stated a similar view. *Cong. Globe.* 31 *Cong.* 1 *Sess.*, I, 369.

[68]*New York Tribune*, June 24, 1850.

[69]*Correspondence*, 782.

[70]Hammond wrote him March 5, 1850, "You must be there with your full power." *Correspondence*, 1212.

[71]*South Carolina Triweekly*, May 25, 1850.

say—and I say it boldly—for I am not afraid to say
the truth on any question, that as things now stand,
the Southern States can not with safety remain in
the Union. ''[72]

In his last letter, dated March 10, Calhoun wrote,
''Nothing short of the terms I propose can settle it
finally and permanently. Indeed it is difficult to
see how two peoples so different and hostile can
exist together in one common Union.''[73] Judge
Beverly Tucker of Virginia, an ardent secessionist,
evidently believed that Calhoun had at last made
up his mind that secession was inevitable. On
March 25, 1850, he wrote his nephew, ''That the
action of South Carolina will be determined is abso-
lutely sure. She has been held in check by Calhoun
for seventeen years. Seeing now no room between
him and the grave for any ambitious career, he for
the first time looks on the subject with a single eye,
and his late speech does but give utterance to what
has been in his mind and in the mind of every man in
that State during this time.''[74]

---

[72]*Congressional Globe*, 31 *Cong.*, 1 *Sess.*, I, 462–463. In December, 1851, Foote stated
in a speech that '' I am now perfectly certain that it was the intention of himself (Calhoun)
and a few others closely associated with him to wield,as far as they might find it in their
power to do so, all the machinery of the Nashville Convention for the purpose of setting
up demands in favor of the Southern States alike unjust and unreasonable in themselves
—a compliance with which they could not have confidently expected. I entertain no
doubt also, at this time that he contemplated the breaking up of the Confederacy as
more than a probable event, and one to which he began to look forward with a good deal
of eagerness.'' *Cong. Globe*, 32 *Cong.*, 1 *sess.* *Appendix*, 51. For Rhetts denial see
Ibid, 61.

The correspondence of Judge Beverly Tucker of Virginia to Ex-Governor Jas. H.
Hammond of South Carolina, both of whom were delegates to the Nashville Convention,
during the spring of 1850, shows that there were those who wished to use the Convention,
to force secession. Tucker desired that demands should be made on the North that
should be so extreme that they would not be accepted. See Tucker's letters of January
27, February 8, 1850, in *Jas. H. Hammond Manuscripts*, Vol. 17, Library of Congress.

[73]*Correspondence*, 784.

[74]*William and Mary Quarterly*, XVIII, 44–46. Tucker wrote Ex-Governor Hammond
May 7, 1850, Calhoun ''died nobly, and his last act redeems all the errors of his life
. . . .I have heard of those who rejoiced in his death as providential. I hope it may
prove so, but not in the way intended by them. They considered him as the moving
cause of excitement in South Carolina. You and I know that he restrained it and restrained himself. When he went home in March 1833, he was prepared to say all that
he said in his last speech and much more, had others been prepared to hear it. I know
it from his own lips.'' *Hammond Manuscript*, Vol. 17.

It would seem that Calhoun was now almost convinced that secession was a necessary measure, but apparently hoped to the last for the preservation of the Union on the terms he had proposed. A few days before his death he dictated an incomplete draft of certain resolutions on the territorial question then at issue.[75] These were directed chiefly against the admission of California under the proposed constitution. It characterized the suggested action as more objectionable than the Wilmot Proviso because "it would effect indirectly and surreptitiously what the proviso proposes to effect openly and directly."[76] The series concluded as follows:—"Resolved, "That the time has arrived when the said Southern States owe it to themselves and the other States comprising the Union, to settle fully and forever all the questions at issue." Calhoun may have intended this draft for use in the Senate or more probably for the Nashville Convention, but they do not seem to have influenced the text of the resolutions adopted by the latter body.[77] His death, occuring two months prior to its meeting left the shaping of the course of the Convention to other and less skilful hands.

Owing to the developments in Congress, the movement for the Convention lost importance and support in the South, and the assembling of its members on the 3rd of June aroused little interest in the North as its action had been discounted. Representatives from nine states were present. The body being composed of seventy-five members from eight states, and one hundred from Tennessee. The Convention was organized with the choice of Judge Sharkey as President. He made a pacific speech, but it probably

---

[75] *Correspondence*, 785–787.

[76] A similar view in his letter of January 4, 1850, Calhoun, *Correspondence*, 779–780.

[77] Joseph A. Scoville, wrote James H. Hammond, April 18, 1850, as follows:—"Mr. Calhoun commenced dictating some resolutions a few days before he died—he did not finish them, whether he intended them for the Senate or for Nashville, I never knew." *Hammond Manuscript*, Vol. 17.

did not express the attitude of the majority of the
delegates. A Committee on Resolutions consisting
of two from each state reported a series of resolutions
based on those presented by John A. Campbell of
Alabama, afterward Justice of the Supreme Court
of the United States, which were adopted unanimously
on a vote by states. These were rather moderate
in character. In fact Colquitt of Georgia characterized them as "tame." The resolutions condemned
the Wilmot Proviso and the other proposed hostile
measures, omitting all mention of the admission of
California. They demanded the extension of the
Missouri Compromise line to the Pacific. This was
pronounced "as an extreme concession" and soon
came to be regarded as the ultimatum of the Convention. They declined "to discuss the methods suitable
for resistance to measures not yet adopted, which
might involve a dishonor to the South," and voted
to re-convene six weeks after the adjournment of
Congress, in case it failed to comply with its demands.[78]

An address to the people of the Southern States,
prepared by R. Barnwell Rhett of South Carolina,
was also reported and aroused much discussion.
It was far more radical than the resolutions, comprising the "choicest specimens of disunion tenets,"
as one of the southern Whig papers remarked.[79]
The Southron declared that neither Calhoun, Hayne
nor McDuffie, "even in the palmiest days of ultra
nullification, ever conceived anything to surpass it."[80]
The address denounced expressly the Compromise

[78]*Journal of Proceedings of the Southern Convention*, 3–8. See S. L. Sioussat, Tennessee, The Compromise of 1850 and the Nashville Convention, in the *Mississippi
Valley Historical Review*, II, 330–340, 343–346, for excellent account of the proceedings
of the two sessions of the Convention. T. D. Herndon, The Nashville Convention of
1850, in *Alabama Historical Society, Transactions* V, 216–233. Cleo. Hearon, Mississippi and The Compromise of 1850, in *Publications of Mississippi Historical Society*,
XIV, ch. VI. Farrar Newberry, The Nashville Convention and Southern Sentiment
of 1850, *South Atlantic Quarterly*, XI, 259–273.

[79]*Southron*, June 28.
[80]*Southron*, June 28.

measures pending in Congress and expressed the belief that sooner or later disunion must come. An earnest attempt was made by the Whigs and a few conservative Democrats to strike out this section, and especially the statement in the address that it would be unconstitutional to admit California. A number of strong speeches were made in opposition to this portion of the address. Beverly Tucker, Professor of Law in the College of William and Mary, however, made a fiery speech in favor of secession.[81] The address was carried by a unanimous vote by states, but on motion the votes of each member were recorded, and from that it appeared that the Whigs were opposed, while most of the Democrats supported it.[82] After a session of nine days, the first session of the Convention adjourned on June 12th. The North by this time, refused to take the Convention seriously. A Philadelphia paper declared, "the prospect is that the members have each made good an excellent claim to ridicule for life."[83] The South, however, regarded it quite differently. The Whigs generally repudiated it, agreeing with *The Republican Banner and Nashville Whig* that the spirit of the Convention and the propositions discussed savor so strongly of disunion that every friend of the Republic must feel that its perpetuity is threatened."[84] On the other hand, the Democrats and Democratic press praised its work and influence.

We are convinced that a careful study of the Southern Convention movement must lead to the conclusion that it was of much greater importance and a more serious menace to the Union than has been generally recognized by many historians. Mr.

---

[81]*Remarks of Beverly Tucker, Southern Convention*, 16 pages, n. d. Copy in Virginia State Library.

[82]*Republican Banner and Nashville Whig*, June 12, 13, 14, 15. This paper said July 4, "only some dozen or fifteen Whigs to some eighty Democrats."

[83]*North American*, quoted by *National Intelligencer*, June 20.

[84]June 17.

Rhodes states that "the Nashville Convention deserves mention more from the hopes and fears it had excited than from its active or enduring effects.[85] While this is true, it is also true, as he points out in another passage "that had the Wilmot Proviso passed Congress, or had slavery been abolished in the District of Columbia, the Southern Convention . . . . would have been a very different affair, from the one that actually assembled at Nashville."[86]

This, it is believed, is apparent from the facts that have been presented. The South, it is clear, would have been united without distinction of party against any such measures. Their various legislative resolutions against the Wilmot Proviso, for example, were not mere gasconade, but represented a deepseated spirit of resistance that undoubtedly would have led to bold and concerted measures to disrupt the Union and to the formation of a Southern Confederacy. But this movement, for the time being, was checked by the passage of the Compromise measures.

While it is undoubtedly true that the project for a Southern Convention and the threat of secession was largely a movement of the politicians rather than one emanating from the people, it is equally true that the Compromise of 1850 was the work of politicians, which was soon to be rejected by the people of both sections. Even at the adjournment of Congress it was not certain that the lower South would accept the Compromise. The Nashville Convention, less representative than when it met in June, convened for a second session from November 11 to 19, 1850. All the delegates who accepted the Compromise measures were absent. The extremists being in control, after a series of disunion speeches had been delivered, adopted a set of radical resolutions. These formally affirmed the right of secession, denounced

---

[85]*History of the United States*, I, 174.
[86]*Ibid*, I, 135.

the recent Compromise Acts of Congress, and recommended a general Congress or Convention of the slave-holding states "with a view and intention of arresting further aggression, and if possible of restoring the constitutional rights of the South and if not, to provide for their safety and independence."[87] But what was more alarming was the very definite movement for immediate secession in the four states of Georgia, Mississippi, Alabama, and South Carolina, which was with difficulty temporarily checked,[88] but not before the agitation had familiarized the people of the South with this remedy for their grievances and strengthened their belief in secession as a constitutional right, thus preparing the way for its adoption a decade later, when the process of the sectionalization of the country had been completed.

---

[87]Cluskey, *Political Text Book*, (2 Ed.) 596–598.

[88]Arthur C. Cole, The South and the Right of Secession in the Early Fifties, *Mississippi Valley Historical Review*, I, 376–399; Cole, *The Whig Party in the South*, ch. VI; Cleo Hearon, *Mississippi and Compromise*, ch. VIII–XII; U. B. Phillips, *Georgia and State Rights*, 161–170. Philip M. Hamer, The Session Movement in South Carolina, 1848-1852. (Univ. of Penn. Ph. D. thesis, June, 1918.)